RHYMING HEARTS

HARJEET KAUR

I Dedicate this Book to My Lovely Parents

S. Major Singh & Parminder Kaur

Contents

1. In The Search of Love

In the magnificent of this world,
In the power of word.

I search for a love,
As rich as a clove.

Deep breath of warmness,
From forest of kindness.

Love has become a deal,
I doubt how I feel.

• 2 •

My heart is still outdated, it seem.
Believing in true love, to find which I am keen.

I don't feel myself compatible,
With the rules of today's love,
Coming on arrival.
My search always continue,
From one guy to another,
Learning colours of attitude.

My heart is still hopeful,
For finding a man soulful.

Stubborn I may be,
But,
I still don't believe,
In the love of 'treat'.

I still believe in a heart for a heart,
Away a second or miles apart.

•4•

It may be a joke or may be a fantasy,
For some,
I believe what is known as materialistic.

Practical hopes,
Practical life & practical world,
Shall exist,
But my search for true love,
True feelings & true warmth,
Shall also persist.

• 5 •

Giving heart to someone forever,
With a bond of trust and love,
Remains still a dream of Harjeet.

In the search of true love,
I still keep my journey on,
Till I reach my man, I will look upon.

2. Ocean of Love

In the ocean of love,
Diving deep in your eyes,
Where my self lies.

A pretty smile on your face,
My smile always chase.

Saute of seriousness,
Silence covered careness.

A warm hug makes my day,
Always take my heart,
The way you slay.

Cute mixed hot,
That's what make me caught.

Imagining all this with you,
I wish to meet soon.

Penning down my feelings,
For a patient healing.

3. A Reluctance

Wished to write another life,
Another beginning.

I know what you are going to say,
The 'roses' you are going to lay.

Wished to write another life,
Another beginning with you.
Where I have lots of happiness to give you.

Don't want to give,
My pains and sufferings.

Year by year,
Love for you in my heart grew.
But,
Day by day,
Life became bitter for me.

With which right I would say you to love me?
Can't ruin your life.
Your smiling playful face.

Wished to write another life,
Another beginning with you,
So that I can love you,
Much beyond I can.

Harjeet don't want to run,
It will be what God planned.

4. Pending Wishes

On the most beautiful day of your life,
On the day whole world is wishing you.
On your special day, I miss to call you and
congratulate.

I know you are super busy,
And I am also boasting that I will wait.

Deep inside I am super jealous,
Feeling last in the queue & the queue is of
infinite persons.

I want to support you the way you say,
Or nay.

I wish I could tell you,
I looked at my phone whole day,
Waiting for your call back.

I wish I could tell you,
I expected a minute call today.

I wish I could tell you,
I too prayed for you each day.

I wish I could tell you,
I too had happiness tears on your every success.

In monkey wrenches I got,
I want to support you,
I will wait for you,
I want to talk to you.

5. For an Adorable Smile

• 15 •

For an adorable smile,
For an adorable person,
Whose adorable laughter matters a lot.

From the beginning of friendship,
On the way ahead,
There's been ups and downs,
Happiness and fights.

There are forgetting moments,
There are forgiving moments.

Though there might be some cringes,
But feelings of heart never changes.

Life is to go on,
Not to stay stagnant on bugging matter.

Inner self never fails to say,
Your smile is much bigger,
Than my temporary anger.

• 17 •

Your laughter is much bigger,
than my temporary complaints.

For an adorable smile,
Which matters a lot.

It's always important to hug the innocence,
After a day of silence,
For a night of immense love.

6. Concealed

A cute face,
Which suddenly got concealed.

For an out of the world guy,
Whose habits are a mystery.

Sending him some love,
And a question to be answered.

Why he is quiet?
And made me out of sight.

Will continue this further,
Only after he replies.

And Harjeet will tell him how dear he was becoming,
With pending signs.

7. A Journey

A journey to meet a special stranger,
A journey to meet, who tingled my heart.

Covering miles away from home,
Just to see a guy I had crush on.

Been months unfruitful,
And now the last day here soon.

Some credit to misunderstandings,
Some credit to less communication,
Some credit to over thinking,
Plans didn't go the way they should.

I kept waiting for him,
And I have no clue what's on his side.

I believe it to be my hurry for coming here,
Covering miles away from home,
Just to see a guy, who went invisible from the
day I stepped here.

I don't know what my future holds,
But,
Till now I regret my decision from soul.

Months of waiting for a guy,
Who just proved himself again and again,
For being an escalator.

Regretting and waiting these months,
Oddly,
Became a new normal.

8. A Wait

His eyes said he loves me,
His text said he doesn't.

Talking with him after months,
And witnessing his disappearance again.

A wait,
Is it worth?
His expression is still a dearth.

• 24 •

Appearing with same feels,
And disappearing with no clues.

A wait,
Is it worth?

• 25 •

His face never denied, the affection in his heart,
His warmth never denied, the reception of his arms.

His sudden disappearance again, raised a question,
Is it worth?

To wait for a man,
Whose eye showed a blinking heart,
Whose action said it was all for a moment.

Years of 'appearance' and disappearance of
months,
Is it worth to wait for him?

Or should I move on away from him?

A hesitation to even ask him,
A reluctance which never said goodbye.

A question my heart asks,
Is he worth?

9. A New

Writing this to a man,
Distance with whom is gradually becoming less.

In between his hard terms,
And ruthless talk sessions,
He is becoming a reason to talk alone.

In between his rude insults,
And arrogant behaviour,
He reflects somewhere he has a sweet soul.

• 29 •

Trying to make a place in his heart,
And his life,
An adventurous journey I have listed in my cart.

In need of a secret sharer,
And a special one.
Will he be my that secret sharer special one?

In need of a shoulder to lean on,
Will he lend his shoulder to lean and sleep on?

I can give my all heart and soul to him.
A loyalty beyond his expectation,
In this world full of situation-ship.

• 31 •

Writing this for an arrogant,
Expecting him to say, "That's my magic Harjeet!"
Indeed something I have started being fond of.
I am ready to bow down honourably before his each word.

In hope of a promising future,
and a love for me in his eyes and his world.

10. And then I decided to wait

May be he loves me,
May be he doesn't,

But I decided to wait for him.

11. Strange Stranger

For a strange stranger who became a happy reason.
Writing this to tell him,
His place in heart of mine.

But expecting an insecure reply of him.

The very first message he sent as reply, "Thank you, ma'am!"
To the day watching his tonnes of emotions.

• 35 •

His Harjeet remembers him saying,
"I am introvert type, please bear with me!"
It's been years since,
Yes I am bearing him but watching his
handsome looks.

The very first call received from him.
The call was special,
For all his gestures,
Also for the place from where he called.
Indeed I blushed living those moments.

Unpredictable times, messages and things,
He made my soul bling.

Yes, I have laughed 'reasoned' reasonlessly
alone,
Yes, I have saved his photos in my phone.

I still feel shy talking with him,
I still get nervous contacting him.

• 37 •

His just one message to meet,
It used to be a hamper of joy for me.

From touching his long lashes,
Till receiving his warm hug,
I miss being next to him

When I took him in my arms,
He said, "I feel relaxed"
When he slept on my shoulder,
It was a sweet pleasure.

From being blocked,
And banned to send a heart in messages.
I have always missed to tell him,
How special he is to me.

12. A Back Deal

So, it was a childhood old love,
Realized in college.

When I had many to be with,
I chose him.

Expected it to be a fairy tale.

• 40 •

He was then failing in his career's sail,
Tried to get him up,

Pampered & loved him,
To make him reach his shore.

The day outs to the mountains,
Walking through the rains.

Making a future plan together,
Keeping children names.

The one complaint he had,
He occasionally got mad.

For the career choices I made,
A child in me,
He used to hate.

• 43 •

Till he got successful,
And I was struggling tight.

And finally, he said me,
"Who are you, Harjeet?
Not going to accept you,
Till you reach my level,
Or things will end up in upheaval!"

I tried to convince him,
Things will get better one day.

Credit to my repeated failures,
He said I don't have time to waste.

It ended up in a major heart break,
A person I admired for long,
Abruptly caused the ache.

13. Moved On

Then I moved on,
From all the tears he gave,
From all the heart breaks he gifted me.

To open new doors.

Causing myself more pain,
Was definitely not my choice.

He did what he intended to,
He did what he actually had in himself.

• 47 •

A deal of emotions,
Till terms and conditions accepted,

Might it be a destiny,
Might it be for a good sake.

Relieving myself from the one,
Who was actually not the one.

14. Denial

He came to meet,
Before starting a new chapter of his life.

I could not meet him,
It was my denial.

For all the injuries and heartbreaks, he gave,
In return of a precious single seat,
I gave in my heart's place.

He was criticizing me,
Waiting at the gate.

How could I allow him again?
My all efforts he threw once in vain.

He was standing to make his final decision.
So, I allowed him to make!

Not choosing me but to choose the girl,
The very next day he proposed,
For marrying him.

I did not allow him,
To take me for sake again.

I did not allow him,
To make my eyes wet again.

I did not allow him,
To speak anything out of his mouth again.

And I did allow him,
To make me broke again.

• 51 •

He had control over my life,
Till I allowed him.

How could I have allowed him,
To abuse that again?

And I bid him farewell on the call,
For a beautiful journey would fall,
With his next day girl.

15. A Little Meet

• 52 •

A little meet with someone,
They call it friends and some benefits.

Future, no.
Hope, no.
This is what the scope is, know.

He became important.

• 53 •

He was the one I was able to open up with,
He was the one I called daily and talked with.

He used to laugh at my sudden expressions,
And I used to hang him up in between my
decisions.

But this journey was meant to end,
Being good friends,
And a respectful journey ahead.

16. Winding Up

Winding up here,
I have not found yet,
The guy I would love endlessly.

May be this would be rhyming heart of every
girl,
Who still finds a heart,
To speak herself.

Beyond intimate needs,
She needs someone.

To wipe her tears,
To give her his ears.

To make her feel secured,
To make her smile ensured.

May be she needs someone,
Who keeps her as one,
In his love & life.

May be this journey continues for her too,
To meet the man she is worth of.